Industrial Locomotives of the

by Ian Brodie

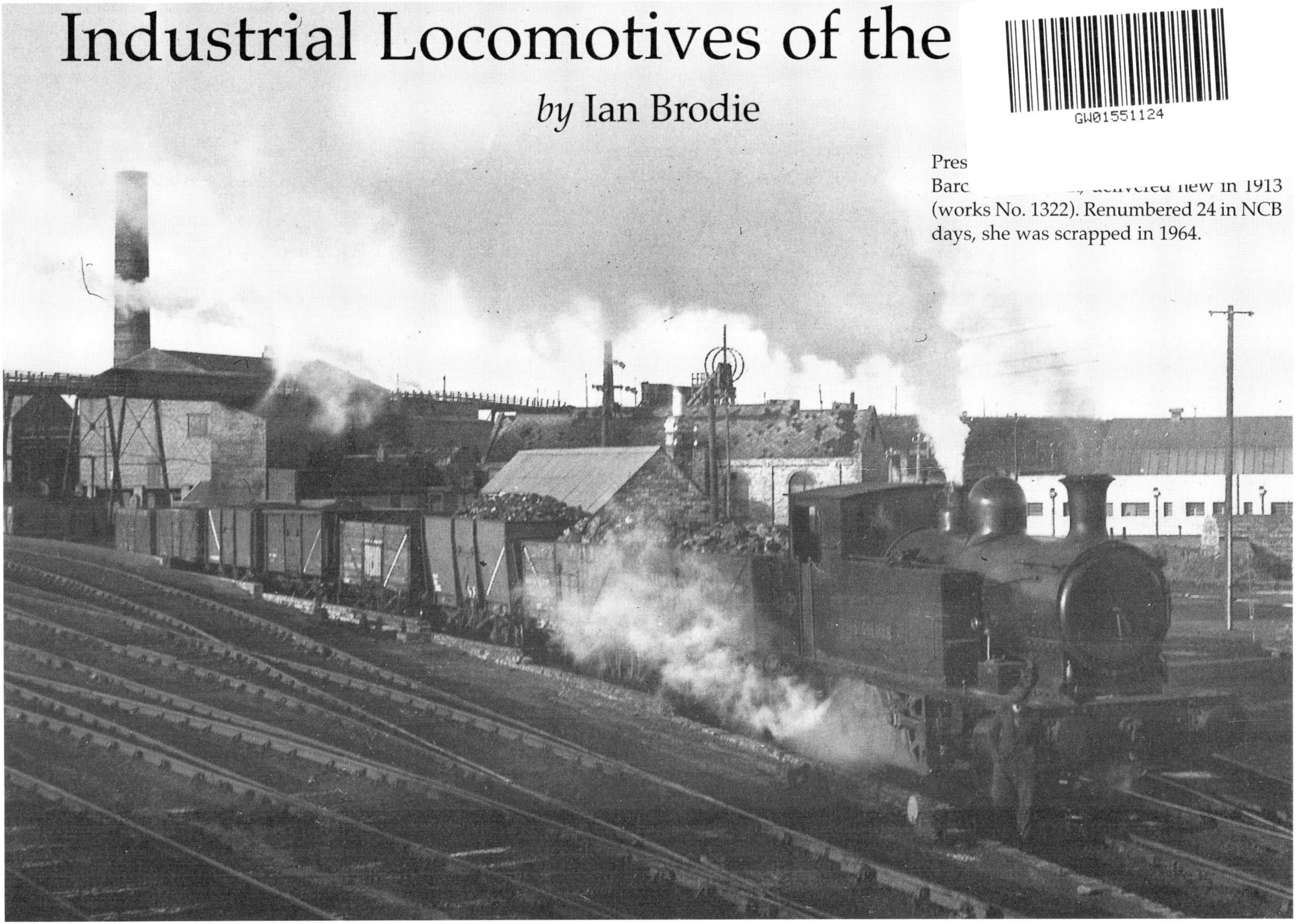

Pres... Barc... delivered new in 1913 (works No. 1322). Renumbered 24 in NCB days, she was scrapped in 1964.

Text © Ian Brodie, 2006.
First Published in the United Kingdom, 2006
Stenlake Publishing Limited
54–58 Mill Square
Catrine
KA5 6RD
www.stenlake.co.uk

ISBN 9781840333886

The publishers regret that they cannot supply
copies of any pictures featured in this book.

Newbattle No. 1 was supposedly built there in 1927. However, she looks every bit a standard Barclay so was presumably assembled from a number of parts which were available. She was briefly at Arniston in 1959, but soon returned to Newbattle where she remained until scrapped on site in April 1970.

INTRODUCTION

Industrial locomotives are still in use today at the giant cement factory south of Dunbar. But this is the exception and in general they are an endangered species, most likely to be found on a preserved railway or on display in a public park. When British Railways was formed on 1 January 1948, it inherited some 20,000 locomotives and it was thought that a similar number existed in industry across the UK. At that time in the Lothians there were about 100 industrial locomotives, operating in approximately 58 separate locations. Of these locomotives, 75% had been built in Kilmarnock, 90% of these at the Caledonia Works of Andrew Barclay, Sons & Co. Ltd. This company is still in existence in Kilmarnock under the name of Hunslet-Barclay Ltd, offering a wide range of engineering and rail–related products. The other Kilmarnock builders Grant, Ritchie & Co. also manufactured heavy equipment such as winding engines for the pits and produced their last Scottish-based locomotive in 1920. Another builder was Gibb & Hogg of Airdrie, but they ceased locomotive production in 1915.

This book features a sample of the different locomotives in use in locations throughout the Lothians, working from east to west - coincidentally starting with the oldest loco extant in the 1940s, then round the East Lothian and Midlothian coal fields and their extension into Edinburgh at Niddrie. Once so productive, some of these pits were closed in the 1950s, most of the rest following by 1965. Woolmet and Newcraighall pits closed between 1966 and 1968 and last to go was the Lady Victoria complex at Newbattle in 1972.

Modern collieries were opened at Monktonhall around 1967 and at Bilston Glen a few years later. NCB locos worked Monktonhall in the late 1960s, but working subsequently passed to British Railways. Four diesel locos were in use at Bilston Glen. Both pits were worked out by the 1980s and closed around the end of that decade. A Workers' Cooperative took over Monktonhall in June 1992, but it was not successful and the pit flooded in 1997. The buildings were demolished shortly afterwards.

There were a number of other locomotive owners in Edinburgh, including the gas works, the Lighting and Cleansing Department, a local foundry, a contractor, a distillery, an electric manufacturer and a papermill. They all lost their rail connections from 1952 onwards, the last to go (with diesel locos) being the North British Distillery in Fountainbridge in 1974.

The heaviest concentration of industry was in West Lothian, where both the large shale oil field, with its various oil works, and the fringe of both the Lanarkshire and Fife coalfields had to be serviced. There was also a naval yard, a distillery, steel foundries, and a substantial number of other factories. The shale oil industry closed down completely in the late 1950s. Severance of rail connections to other industries commenced in 1961. Among the last rail connections to go were the steel foundries in Armadale and Bathgate, the MOD depot at Dalmeny, and the British Leyland tractor factory in Bathgate. All of these latterly used diesel locomotives. Many of the smaller collieries were closed in the 1950s, but Kinneil at Bo'ness was expanded and joined up with the Fife coalfield. It blossomed until the opening of Longannet power station in Fife, when the coal was diverted to serve it. The colliery closed in 1981. Polkemmet, on the moors above Whitburn, was flooded during the miners' strike in 1983, and never reopened. It was the last working colliery in West Lothian.

In 1947 I received a new bicycle, and armed with my father's 25-year-old camera, set off on various trips to the industrial scenes in East and Midlothian. A great adventure was the trip I took west to Winchburgh to view the electric railway. These photographs form the backbone of this book and I have been very fortunate in having them accompanied by images from the collections of two friends whose contributions are acknowledged below.

Acknowledgements

My thanks go to the following for contributing photographs to this book: Alan Brotchie for the back cover and pages 7 (G. Alliez collection), 8 (*upper*), 11, 12 (G. Alliez collection), 14, 16 (*upper*), 18, 25 and 26 (both Doug Beath collection), 29, 39, 41 (a & b) (both G. Alliez collection), and front cover (G. Alliez collection); and Hamish Stevenson for pages 24 (E.S. Lomax collection), 27, 31-33, 38 (Industrial Railway Society – collection of Jim Peden), 40 (*lower*) (E.S. Lomax collection), 42 (G. Alliez collection), 33–48. Thanks also to John Burnie for providing access to the information which allowed the history of the locomotives and their places of work to be included. All attempts have been made to contact the copyright holders of the photographs appearing in this book; please contact the publishers if further information is required.

EAST LOTHIAN

At the investment of the National Coal Board on 1 January 1947, the Summerlee Iron Co. Ltd of Coatbridge contributed Prestongrange Colliery to the new organisation. This was connected to the East Coast Main Line by a three-quarter mile steeply graded line to sidings one mile south west of Prestonpans Station, and also ran around the derelict Morrison's Haven harbour to sea spoil tips. The colliery was closed in December 1962. The main building, with a fine beam pumping engine, remains as the central feature of the Prestongrange Industrial Heritage Museum. In 1947 Prestongrange had a fleet of four locomotives, one brand new, the other three positive antiques! The oldest, No. 6 (pictured here), was out of use by that time so the colliery actually had a fleet of only three working locomotives. No. 6 dated from 1869 (Andrew Barclay works No. 88), had originally worked at the Coatbridge Ironworks, and was transferred to Prestongrange in 1895. It is noted as rebuilt in 1883 and 1897, and was sold for scrap to J.N. Connel Ltd of Coatbridge around 1952.

No. 2 was acquired by Prestongrange from a contractor working on the Berwick line. She was built in 1884 by the Falcon Engine Co. Ltd of Loughborough and was the only locomotive from this builder employed in Scotland. She is seen here in 1949 working a train of empties from the sea tip. The men on the left have been collecting 'sea coal' from the tip. Like No. 6 she went for scrap to J.N. Connel of Coatbridge around 1952.

No. 3, here seen pounding towards the exchange sidings in 1949, came new from Andrew Barclay's in 1946 (works No. 2219) and handled all the uphill exchange traffic. On the closure of Prestongrange in 1962, she was renumbered 17 and transferred to Lady Victoria Colliery, but she eventually came back home to become part of the collection at the Prestongrange Industrial Heritage Museum. The collection also includes 0-4-2ST No. 7 (Grant Ritchie No. 536 of 1907) and two 0-4-0 Barclays – No. 2043 of 1937, which started life at Bathville, Bathgate, but spent most of her life in Lanarkshire, before finally coming to Kinneil, Bo'ness; and No. 1142 of 1908, which was Fife based during her working life. There are also a number of diesels of Simplex, Ruston & Hornsby, and English Electric manufacture.

Preston Links Colliery at Cockenzie lay at the eastern end of the coalfield and was one of a number of pits owned by Edinburgh Collieries Ltd. It was connected to the East Coast Main Line by a one mile branch to a junction half a mile north east of Prestonpans Station. This colliery was closed in February 1964. Usually two locomotives were based there. No. 3, seen here at some point before nationalisation, was from Andrew Barclay - works No. 989 of 1903. She had previously worked at Wallyford. Renumbered 27, she remained at Preston Links until the colliery closed and she was scrapped in May 1964.

Fleets Colliery, near Tranent, was another owned by Edinburgh Collieries Ltd. Its line ran from Limeylands on the Ormiston line, a mile west of the site of Ormiston Station. The colliery lay one and a half miles north of the branch's junction. The line was extended northwards in the 1920s by some two and a half miles around Tranent to Meadowmill Washery on the East Coast Main Line half a mile north east of Prestonpans Station. Coal from Fleets requiring washing was then brought to Meadowmill while the remainder was sent south via Ormiston. The colliery was closed in March 1959 and the track removed two years later. It had purchased this 4-4-0 tank (right) from the War Department in 1925 and operated her until she was scrapped in January 1935. Built in 1878 by Hudswell Clarke & Rogers Ltd of Leeds, she had began life on the Lynn & Fakenham Railway in Norfolk, later becoming No. 8 on the Midland & Great Northern Railway.

More conventional was Fleets No. 9 (Andrew Barclay works No. 1996 of 1934), photographed at Ormiston North in 1949 after she had been beautifully repainted in the fashion adopted by NCB Lothians Area at that time. Renumbered 29, her base was either Limeylands or Meadowmill (both on the Fleets line), but after the colliery closed she was transferred to Arniston, and later worked at Lady Victoria and the new Bilston Glen Colliery. She was moved to Pittencreiff Park in Dunfermline in the 1990s and is still on display there.

Limeylands Colliery at Ormiston, at the connection with the Fleets line, had been operated by the Ormiston Coal Co. Ltd. The colliery closed about 1953, but a coal preparation plant continued until October 1958. Seen here in 1949 is Ormiston Coal Co. No. 2 (Andrew Barclay works No. 2146 of 1942). By 1955, and renumbered 31, she was at Niddrie. She returned to Fleets in 1958, before moving to Bellyford (Ormiston) in 1961, Lady Victoria in 1962, Meadowmill in 1964, and returned to Niddrie for scrapping in 1970.

South of Ormiston a 2′ 0″ gauge line ran one mile to Tynemount Colliery (closed in January 1952) and on to Oxenford No. 2 (closed in 1951). This was served by Ruston & Hornsby four wheeled petrol locomotives. A train of coal trucks is seen here at Southend, Oxenford, in 1950. This line had closed by 1954.

MIDLOTHIAN

Edinburgh Collieries Ltd operated two collieries in Midlothian, Wallyford and Carberry. By NCB days Wallyford had become a pumping station and wagon works and closed in 1962. A half-mile branch connected it with sidings on the East Coast Main Line one and half miles north east of Inveresk Station. The loco shown (Andrew Barclay works No. 851 of 1899) had originally been at James Waldie & Sons, Tranent Collieries, but was at Wallyford before nationalisation and remained there until 1960. Spells followed at Meadowmill, Prestongrange, Lady Victoria and Newbattle Coal Stocking Site, where it was scrapped by the Motherwell Machinery & Scrap Co. Ltd in August 1968.

Carberry Colliery was reached by a steeply graded three-quarter mile long branch from the Ormiston line half a mile north of Smeaton Station. The colliery closed on 16 March 1960, though a land sale depot and the rail system remained in use until about 1963. 'Carberry' was delivered new from Andrew Barclay (works No. 930 of 1902) and was rebuilt by Hawthorns of Leith in 1924. Numbered 12, and later 26 by the NCB, she was transferred to Arniston in June 1963 and was scrapped the following March.

Dalkeith Colliery was owned by A.G. Moore & Co. Ltd and was accessed from a 600 yard line from Crossgatehall Station on the Ormiston branch. This was superseded by new sidings, serving new pits at Smeaton, accessed from the one-time Hardengreen line. These were lifted in 1956. Loco No. 11 (previously No. 1 and Andrew Barclay works No. 1262 of 1912) is seen here near Smeaton in 1950. She was scrapped in 1953 when shunting on the new lines was taken over by British Railways.

The Lothian Coal Co. operated the vast complex around Newtongrange, which included the Lady Victoria pit and was accessed by sidings on the east side of the Edinburgh—Hawick line. Also here were the Central Workshops. A branch, running two miles to Easthouses and on for a further mile to a land sale depot, was eventually replaced by a narrow gauge line. Easthouses closed on 3 October 1969 and traffic at Lady Victoria ceased in April 1972. The Lady Victoria pit is now the site of the Scottish Mining Museum. Loco No. 3 had been built by Hawthorns of Leith in 1880. No information is available as to her length of service, but a new No. 3 was in use by 1920.

Newbattle No. 3 (Andrew Barclay works No. 1458 of 1916) was built for the Ministry of Munitions and used at a depot in Houston, Paisley, until that closed in 1919. She became the only six-coupled locomotive in use at Lady Victoria, although four 0-4-2STs were in use. One of these (Grant Ritchie No. 536 of 1914) is now preserved at the Prestongrange Museum. A similar locomotive is shown on page 47 at Polkemmet in 1968. No. 3 is seen here in March 1950, spotlessly clean. Apart from a brief visit to Preston Links in 1959, she remained at Lady Victoria until the site closed in 1972.

Right: Diesel locomotives were introduced at Lady Victoria in the 1950s. This is the builder's photograph of No. 10 (Andrew Barclay works No. 414 of 1957). She was moved to Monktonhall Colliery in 1965 and to Bilston Glen four years later.

Left: Arniston Colliery, Gorebridge, had been the property of the Arniston Coal Co. It accessed the Hawick line by a half-mile branch to sidings half a mile west of Gorebridge Station. The pit closed on 29 April 1962, the washery being retained for another year after which the site became a store for withdrawn machinery. The rail connection was lifted around 1965. No. 7 was a powerful 0-6-0, delivered new to Arniston in 1923 from Manning, Wardle & Co. Ltd of Hunslet, Leeds (works No. 1917) and was the last new locomotive built for Arniston. With a short wheelbase, high boiler and squat saddletank clear of the firebox, her appearance was quite different to the Barclays. Renumbered 10, she transferred to Lady Victoria in 1957 and was scrapped the same year. She is seen here in March 1950.

All three Arniston locos were six coupled, the other two being Barclays. This 1949 picture shows No. 6 (Andrew Barclay works No. 1233 of 1911) running light. Renumbered 9, she had transferred via Newbattle to Niddrie by 1961, where she was scrapped on site in September 1969. Arniston's other loco, No. 5 (Andrew Barclay works No. 1175 of 1909), still exists as a static display at Polkemmet Country Park, West Lothian, and is illustrated on the inside back cover.

P. Mitchell & Sons Ltd ran the Esperton Limeworks, reached by a three-mile branch running south south-west from Fushiebridge Station on the Hawick line. In addition to a standard gauge line, there was a narrow gauge system, which operated from 1862 until 1941. The works were closed and dismantled in 1942. This illustration shows the first 2′ 8″ gauge loco, 'Mountaineer', delivered from Hawthorns of Leith in 1862. She was scrapped in 1906.

MIDLOTHIAN

CITY OF EDINBURGH

The Niddrie & Benhar Coal Co. Ltd had an extensive rail system. From workshops at Niddrie, and connection to Steel's bathroom factory, it connected with the Edinburgh Suburban & South Side line one and a half miles from Duddingston Station. Southwards, it ran past the brickworks uphill for one and a half miles to Woolmet Colliery, and eastwards a half mile to Newcraighall Colliery. The Woolmet line closed in September 1966, followed by Newcraighall on 25 May 1968.The workshops had closed in 1959 and use of locomotives ceased in December 1972. In 1947 there were five locomotives - two 0-4-0s and three 0-6-0s - and four of these locos were by Andrew Barclay. The fifth locomotive was No. 4 (Gibb & Hogg No. 54 of 1904) and it is seen here on 24 April 1947 crossing the main road into the workshops area. Renumbered 18 and loaned at times to Limeylands & Prestongrange, she was at Niddrie when scrapped in April 1961.

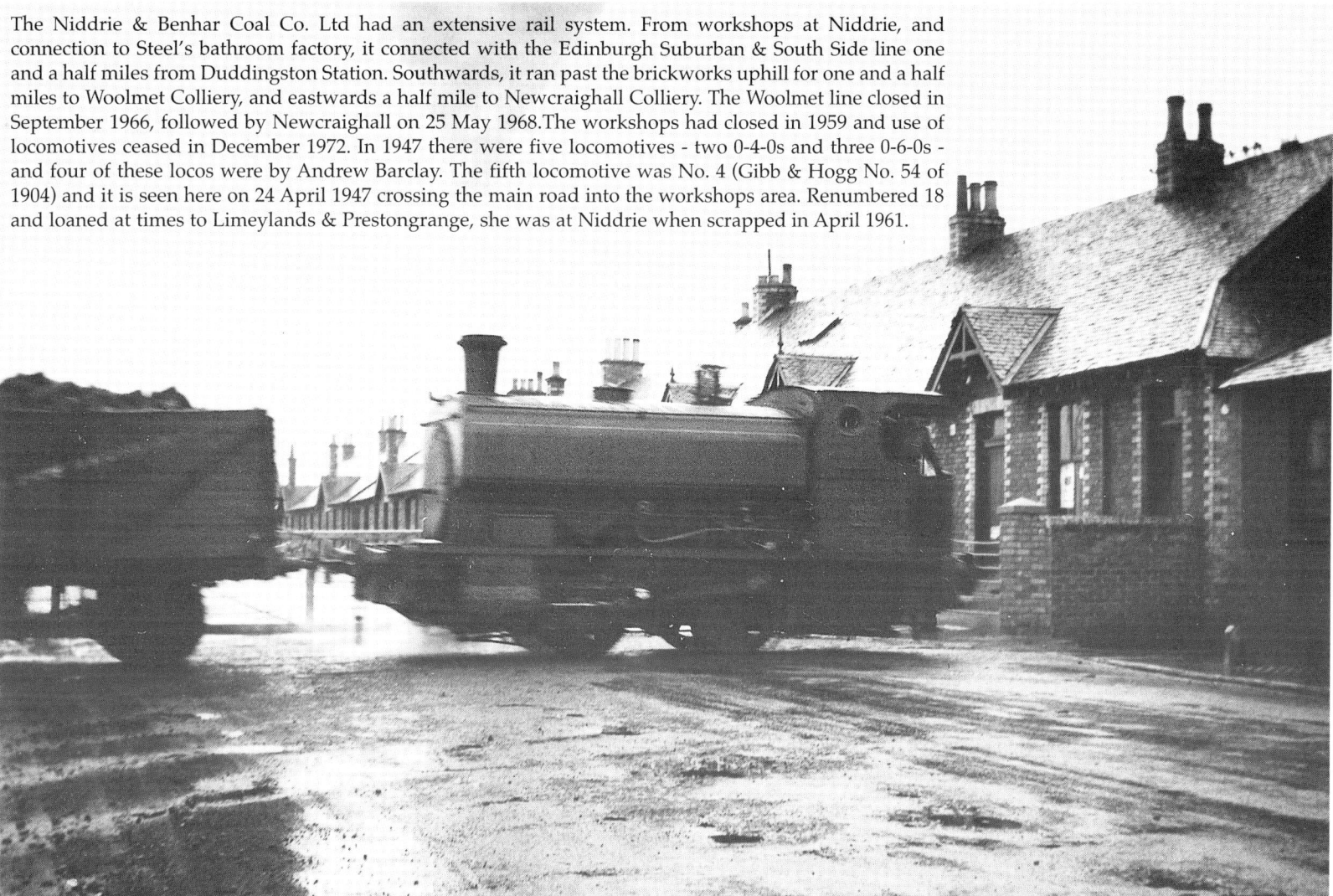

Left: No. 5 (Andrew Barclay works No. 1244 of 1911), leaving Steel's factory in 1948. Renumbered 19, she was scrapped on site in October 1971.

Below: Lunchtime at Niddrie, 1950, and No. 6 (Andrew Barclay works No. 1833 of 1924) and No. 4 sit sizzling below the engine shed. The locos always faced uphill and Woolmet workings were made with the loco at the downhill end to avoid any runaway wagons. Nos. 6 and 7 were big engines with 16" x 24" cylinders and 3' 7" wheels. They had a ferocious 'bark' and, when pushing a train up to Woolmet, could be heard miles away! Renumbered 20 and occasionally loaned to Preston Links and Meadowmill, No. 6 was transferred to Newbattle in 1969 where she latterly lay out of use.

Niddrie No. 7 (Andrew Barclay works No. 2026 of 1937) under repair at Niddrie, May 1948. Renumbered 21 she was withdrawn in September 1969. Purchased for preservation, after a period at Leith she was moved to the Strathspey Railway where she remains today, although she is not currently in use. Another similar locomotive, No. 25, was delivered new from Barclay's in 1954 (works No. 2358). She was transferred to Polkemmet when Niddrie closed in December 1972.

Granton Gasworks' rail system was accessed off the Caledonian branch from Murrayfield to Granton. This was owned by Edinburgh Corporation Gas Dept. until 1 May 1949, when it was nationalised as part of the Scottish Gas Board. There were four standard gauge four-wheeled Barclays at the time of nationalisation. This is No. 10 (works No. 1890 of 1926) in use on 3 August 1947. Loaned to Falkirk Gasworks from 1961–3, she then returned to Granton, until purchased for preservation and moved to the Strathspey Railway. She is not currently in use.

There was also a 2' 0" gauge system at Granton, with two locomotives, specifically for working under the gas retorts. This is No. 5, built by Andrew Barclay as works No. 988 of 1903. She had been rebuilt at Granton in 1912 and is seen here on the same day as No. 10 (opposite). She was sold about 1960 to J.H. Farr of Wardie Garage, Ferry Road, Edinburgh, and displayed there until moved to his 'museum' at Fox Covert Drive in September 1963. On his death she became the property of the National Museum of Scotland and was displayed at Biggar Gasworks for a number of years. On the gasworks' privatisation, No. 5 was moved to the museums store at Granton.

The contractor A.M. Carmichael had a depot at West Craigs, Corstorphine, and locos not in use would be stored here. Seen here is the 3′ gauge side tank, Andrew Barclay works No. 1173 of 1909. She had seen use at the building of a tunnel at Portobello Power Station in 1929–31, then in 1932 worked on the construction of the Ballachulish–Fort William–Inverness road. Employment at the Carsphairn Dam in Galloway followed in 1934–36. She was offered for sale in May 1938, but was not sold and presumably then languished at the West Craigs Depot. She had been scrapped by May 1951.

Bruce Peebles & Co. Ltd, electrical engineers of Granton, had a short branch accessed from the Caledonian Leith North branch at East Pilton Station. They had built their sole locomotive themselves in 1903 and, as befitted their trade, it was electrically powered from tramway style overheads. The photograph shows two transformers being conveyed into the works. The loco was scrapped in 1961 when the overhead system was dismantled and shunting carried out by diesel crane. The connecting Leith North branch closed on 4 September 1967.

Another industry served by an electric system was Kinleith Papermills at Currie, owned by Henry Bruce & Sons Ltd, which was connected to the Caledonian's Balerno branch by an uphill 1 in 50 gradient. The mills had one electric locomotive, built by Thomas Parker Ltd of Wolverhampton about 1895, which operated on double overhead wires as used later with trollybuses. The mill closed in 1966, the electric loco having been scrapped shortly before.

The Royal Naval Victualling Yard at Dalmeny had a rail connection to the main line to the Forth Bridge and had its own locomotive (diesel from 1948). The yard was also used as a store for unwanted items from other naval depots. The yard's six-coupled pannier tank, No. 7 'Forth', is seen here – out of use - on 14 September 1958 at her previous home of Rosyth Dockyard, where she had been replaced by Planet diesels. 'Forth' had been built by W.G. Bagnell Ltd of Stafford (works No. 2615 of 1940) and was delivered new to Rosyth. She was transferred to the Dalmeny yard in December 1959, remaining there until sold to James Young, contractor of Carmyle, Lanark, in 1973.

The Distillers Co. Ltd at Kirkliston had a rail connection to the Newbridge to Dalmeny branch. Their sole locomotive was this small Barclay (works No. 741 of 1894) which they had acquired from the Ardgowan Distillery, Greenock, in 1933 and which proudly displayed the Greenock address on its tank sides throughout its life. It was scrapped on site in March 1959, having been replaced by a four-wheeled Ruston & Hornsby diesel. It was transferred to Kilmarnock once rail traffic ceased in 1966.

Fison's Ltd at Bo'ness (known as the Forth Chemical and Manure Works until 1946) had employed one locomotive since the early 1890s. Latterly, it was this small Barclay (works No. 917 of 1902) which they had purchased from Baird & Stevenson, quarrymasters of Locharbriggs, Dumfries, in July 1948. It was scrapped at Bo'ness in 1961 when rail connection to the factory ceased.

Kinneil Colliery at Bo'ness had been owned latterly by the Kinneil Cannel and Coking Coal Co. Ltd and was directly connected to the Manuel—Bo'ness branch. This shows one of its earlier locomotives, No. 3 (Andrew Barclay works No.1194 of 1910). It was scrapped in 1938.

By 1951 the pit had expanded substantially and in 1964 was linked underground with the Fife coalfield. Most of the combined output was brought up at the new preparation plant at Kinneil. Kinneil was isolated from the other West Lothian pits and was managed in NCB days as part of the Fife and later Alloa areas, and remained in the Northern Area until all Scotland was managed as one area from 1973. No. 4 was a product of R. & W. Hawthorn, Leslie & Co. Ltd, Newcastle-upon-Tyne (works No. 3175 of 1916), and had come from I.C.I., Billingham, County Durham. She was scrapped in 1962.

NCB No. 41 (Andrew Barclay works no. 1107, built in 1907) had originally been No. 13 in the fleet of the Lochgelly Iron and Coal Co. Ltd and worked at Minto Colliery in Lochgelly. By 1956 she was at Glencraig Colliery, Lochgelly. She came to Kinneil in 1967 and is seen there on 19 February 1968. She was scrapped at Airdrie in January 1972.

There was also a 2' gauge system at Kinneil and this photograph shows the four-wheeled diesel mechanical loco in action on 10 February 1969. She is a Ruston & Hornsby of Lincoln, works No. 283868 of 1949, delivered new to Torry Mine at Newmills, Fife, and transferred to Kinneil in 1961. No. 47 (Andrew Barclay works No. 2157 of 1943) is in the background. She had come to the Fife Coal Co. from the Royal Ordnance Factory in Swynnerton, Staffordshire, in November 1946 and, after working in a number of Fife locations, came to Kinneil in December 1968. Kinneil's fortunes nosedived with the opening of Longannet Power Station in Fife. In the summer of 1978 the underground conveyors were connected to the Longannet complex and the flow reversed so that the coal emerged by the new power station. By 1981 the colliery had closed, along with the branch line to Manuel. The Scottish Railway Preservation Society now operate this line as the Bo'ness & Kinneil Railway.

Left: The Oakbank Oil Co. Ltd operated the shale processing works at Winchburgh. A 2' 6" gauge overhead electric line connected this with a mine near Newton, one and a half miles north. From there the line continued westwards for a further one and a half miles as a cable-hauled tramway to a mine at Whitequarries, where Dougal Phillip's New Hopetoun Garden Centre now stands. The original locos, Nos. 1 and 2, were American, products of the Baldwin Locomotive Works in Philadelphia and were delivered new in 1902. No. 2 passed to the Royal Scottish Museum, who currently have it in store, while No. 1 was scrapped in November 1961, after the line had closed on 17 February 1961. The photograph shows one of them approaching the Winchburgh road bridge in 1950.

Above: The Oakbank Oil Co.'s No. 3 came from Westinghouse, but its place or date of build are unknown. She is here seen shunting in the yard at Winchburgh in May 1950. She too was scrapped in 1961.

The Oakbank Co.'s Nos. 5 and 6 were products of a joint venture between Metropolitan Vickers Electrical Co., Manchester, and Andrew Barclay of Kilmarnock, and the locos were built in 1942 and 1946 respectively. This photograph shows a train stopped just below the main road bridge at Winchburgh. It includes the workers' coaches towards the rear, although it looks as though most of the miners travelled on top of the loaded shale trucks. These two locomotives were sold to Connell of Coatbridge in 1961.

NO-626

PHILPSTOUN OIL WORKS
Nº 2

The oil works at Pumpherston, Broxburn, Oakbank and Philipstoun merged with Young's Oil Company to form Scottish Oils in 1920, with headquarters at Middleton Hall in Uphall. Many of the previous owners' names remained on the locomotives. Philipstoun Oil Works, near Linlithgow, was operated by James Ross & Co. Ltd and had a connection to the Edinburgh—Glasgow main line. This photograph shows No. 2 (Andrew Barclay works No. 1120 of 1907) looking very smart. The loco was scrapped in April 1930 and the works closed in 1934.

The Broxburn–Pumpherston area formed an extensive rail system, sprawling from Uphall east to Broxburn, then north west to Threemiletown and Ecclesmachan, and also south to Roman Camp and Pumpherston. Main line rail connections were made with the Edinburgh—Glasgow line near Winchburgh, and with the Bathgate line at Drumshoreland and the Caledonian's Edinburgh line near Kirknewton. With one exception, the Broxburn Oil Company's eight locomotives were all products of Andrew Barclay's works and all were four-wheelers. This photograph shows No. 5 (works No. 661 of 1890) which was delivered new to the Broxburn Oil Co. In 1940 it was transferred to the Oakbank Oil Co. for service at Gavieside, near West Calder. It was sold to Connell of Coatbridge for scrap in June 1957.

Broxburn Oil Co. No. 6 was a Barclay product of 1897 (works No. 789) and is seen here at Roman Camp Works, near Drumshoreland, in September 1950. It was based there from 1924 until 1956, when it was sold to P. & W. Maclellan of Langholm, Lanarkshire, for scrap. These locomotives had to travel relatively long distances and their coal supply was augmented by attaching four-wheeled wooden tenders, as seen here. Roman Camp Works closed in 1956 and were dismantled over the following two years.

This is Broxburn Oil Co. No.1 (Andrew Barclay works No. 1594 of 1919), possibly at Pumpherston. Delivered new, she operated until 1957 when sold to Dixon's Ironworks in Govan, Glasgow. She was scrapped two years later.

The other company well known in the West Lothian oilfield was Young's Paraffin Light & Mineral Oil Co. Ltd which operated, amongst others, the Hopetoun Oil Works near Winchburgh and the Uphall Oil Works and Shale Mine. These two photographs show Uphall engines.

Upper: No. 7 (Grant Ritchie works No. 522 of 1907), which had been delivered new to Uphall as an 0-4-2 tank. The trailing pony was subsequently removed. She was transferred first to the Hopetoun Works (where she was known as Hopetoun No. 7), then to the Broxburn Oil Co. at Roman Camp in 1953. Coming back to Young's Pumpherston Oil Works in 1958, she went to Barnes & Bell Ltd, Coatbridge, for scrap in 1959. Hopetoun Oil Works closed about 1954, having latterly been worked by locos from Scottish Oils' Middleton Workshops.

Lower: Uphall No. 8 (Andrew Barclay works No. 1152 of 1908), delivered new and initially numbered 2. She was transferred to the Broxburn Oil Co.'s Roman Camp Works in 1936 and in 1955 moved to the Broxburn Works. In 1957 she was sold to Dixon's Ironworks of Govan, Glasgow, and scrapped in 1959.

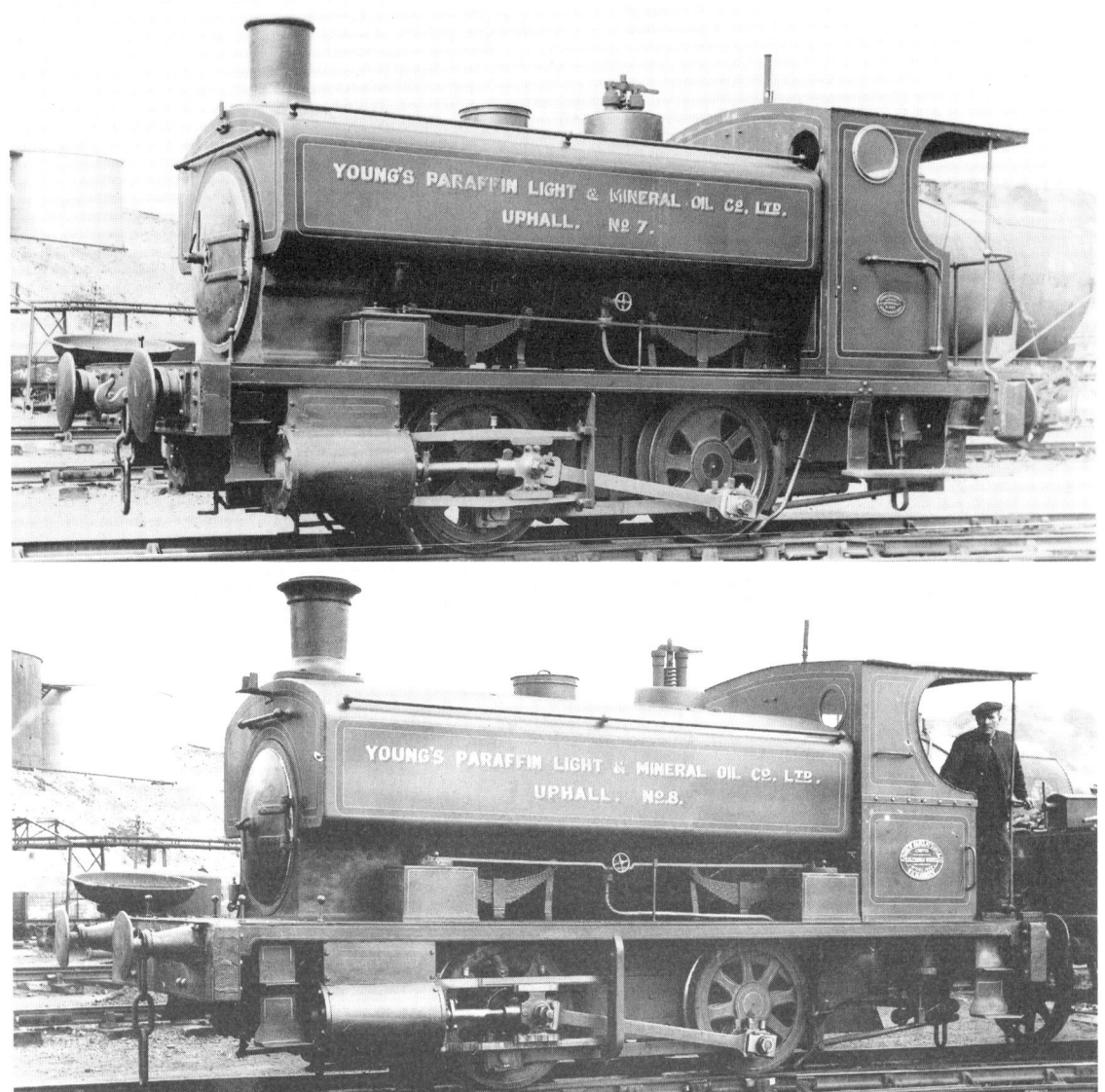

Young's also owned the Addiewell Chemical and Paraffin Works and Shale Mine, together with a number of pits in the area. Seen here is No. 4, a Grant Ritchie product (works No. 698 of 1920). She had been delivered new to the Oakbank Oil Co. for use at the Oakbank Refinery, Midcalder, and was transferred to Young's in 1931. She was later briefly transferred to the Oakbank Oil Co.'s Gavieside Works in 1959 and again about March 1960, and was scrapped on site by Connel of Coatbridge in September 1963.

Addiewell No. 9 (Andrew Barclay works No. 1373 of 1914) came new to the Addiewell Works and was scrapped about 1958. The works were closed in August 1956 and demolished by 1960.

The West Lothian coalfield was at the eastern end of the huge Lanarkshire field. Prior to nationalisation in 1947, many of the collieries had been under the ownership of United Collieries Ltd. This photograph, taken on 8 July 1936, shows their No. 3 which was delivered new to them from Andrew Barclay (works No. 1809 of 1923). Originally based at Bredisholm Colliery, Bargeddie, Coatbridge, she was later at the Bathville Works in Armadale and also at Greenriggs Colliery near Whitburn. Transferred to Shotts Locomotive Works in 1949, she was at Polkemmet (numbered 38) by 1959, going to Easton Colliery, Bathgate, in 1962 during a rail strike when NCB locomotives were temporarily used on internal traffic. These workings reverted to British Railways after the strike and she was then stored at Easton until scrapped about 1966.

WEST LOTHIAN

The former United Collieries No. 6 at Shotts on 19 August 1960. Another Barclay (works No. 948 of 1903), she had worked at Westrigg Colliery, between Blackridge and Armadale on the Bathgate line, and afterwards was based at Bathville Works. In 1947 she went to United Fireclay Products at Armadale, passing into NCB ownership in June 1950. Then employed at Foulshiels Colliery at Stoneyburn, which connected with the Bathgate—Morningside line, she was at Polkemmet in 1951 before briefly returning to Foulshiels in 1955. She then went to Loganlee Colliery, Addiewell, connected to Stoneyburn as above, and operated at one or other of these two locations until moved to Shotts locomotive works in November 1959. She was sold to Connell of Coatbridge for scrap in June 1962.

This fine 0-6-0 tank is United Collieries No. 13 (Andrew Barclay No. 1131 of 1907), delivered new for work at Loganlee Colliery, Addiewell. She was later at Greenrigg Colliery, near Whitburn, returning to Loganlee about 1950. By 1957 she was a Polkemmet engine and remained there until scrapped in December 1963.

This is No. 16, a Gibb & Hogg product of 1898, which was a stalwart at Loganlee pit. Brief work stints were put in at nearby Foulshiels with overhauls at Shotts, until transfer to Cardowan Colliery, Stepps, Lanarkshire, in March 1965. The photograph shows her at Loganlee. She was moved on 8 March 1968 to the Carnegie Memorial Park, Dunfermline, where she was a static display, and around 1990 was moved again to Summerlee Park, Coatbridge, to allow a Coatbridge-built locomotive to be displayed there.

Polkemmet Colliery, high on the moors above Whitburn, was owned prior to nationalisation by William Dixon Ltd of Calder Ironworks near Airdrie. It was connected by a three and a half mile branch with both the Bathgate—Morningside line and the Edinburgh—Holytown line at junctions at Fauldhouse. The lower part of this line was a British Railways branch as far as Benhar Junction, where the exchange sidings were. The colliery locomotives worked for one mile up a 1 in 34 incline to reach there and many trains were double headed. Three locomotives were based there at nationalisation and seen here is No. 15, a Grant Ritchie 0-4-2T (works No. 539 of 1917). It had arrived from Colville's Glengarnock works in Ayrshire in 1935 and remained there for the rest of her working life. This photograph was taken on 4 January 1968, at a time when she was a spare engine. She was subsequently cannibalised to rebuild No. 12 (see page 48) and was scrapped on site in July 1973.

Also taken on 4 January 1968, this photograph shows the older locomotives stored out of use. From right to left are No. 16 (Hudswell Clarke works No. 1331 of 1918) and No. 22 (Andrew Barclay works No. 1007 of 1904). No. 16 had been delivered new to Colvilles Ltd, had been used at Mossend Engineering Works at Bellshill, Lanarkshire, and was purchased by Dixon's for use at Polkemmet in 1935. It was transferred to Killoch Colliery in Ayrshire in November 1969 and was scrapped the following April. No. 22 had worked first in the Motherwell area and then around Twechar and Auchengreich before coming to Polkemmet in December 1965. She was scrapped in July 1973. In the distance are Nos. 8 (previously 14; Andrew Barclay works No. 885 of 1900) and 17 (Hunslet Engine Co., Leeds, works No. 2880 of 1943).

This loco, No. 12 (Andrew Barclay No. 1829 of 1924), was originally of different appearance with a tank that did not cover the smokebox. She was similar to the Niddrie twins (see pages 20/21) and, owned by James Nimmo, worked at Auchengeich Colliery in Lanarkshire and around Twechar. She came to Polkemmet in March 1965, where she was rebuilt in 1970 using the boiler, tank and other parts of Grant Ritchie No. 539 (see page 46). Steam working at Polkemmet ceased in 1980, but No. 12 survived until 1987 when she was cut up on site.